Virgin Heart

FEATURING "LIGHTNING BUGS,"
shedding a little "LIGHT" in dark places

Delores J. Chandler

1663 LIBERTY DRIVE, SUITE 200
BLOOMINGTON, INDIANA 47403
(800) 839-8640
WWW.AUTHORHOUSE.COM

First published by AuthorHouse 01/10/07

ISBN: 1-4208-8635-5 (sc)

Library of Congress Control Number: 2006900085

Printed in the United States of America
Bloomington, Indiana

This book is printed on acid-free paper.

DEDICATION

This book is dedicated to
"LIFE," "LOVE," and the pursuit of "MERCY."

Acknowledgements

A radiance of GOODWILL and THANKS go out to the Creator of all things, the family of God, my husband, peers, associates, family, friends, and nature for their contributions to the completion of this passage.

PREFACE

SPECTROGRAPHICALLY speaking: ENTER congregated viewers, readers, and listeners. The poems, prayers, and revelations embedded in this passage are all my Beloved spiritual children of various ages, ranging from infancy to mature; giving birth to a God-Fearing Mighty Nation. Please handle with care. Ever since Jesus saved me, God's chastisement and compassion always result in me being spiritually impregnated with another praise-filled anointed offspring. Behold, your HOST and our Family.

Lightning Bug #106

Earthly emotions can be shaken and stirred, and the physical being can be broken and bruised; but, THE HOLY GHOST SHALL NOT BE MOVED.

Contents

BEHOLD SATAN

Arise and take heed to the words of the LORD

God has removed the veil that was placed on our eyes from birth. We now see you for what you are. We Renounce all your Filthy, Sinful, and Deceitful ways.

Your unholy services are no longer needed. We COMMAND that you leave us be in PEACE, in the name of JESUS CHRIST, the Son of God; who redeemed our souls and reconciled us with our Creator, who is the Holy God.

BLESSED BE THE NAME OF OUR LORD FOREVERMORE

> You are a MURDERER, a THIEF, and a LIAR; the Author of Confusion, a "Stench" – an ABOMINATION

> You are an Imminent Immoral Destruction of Mankind

> You are a Cheap Imitation of DEITY, HONOR, and POWER

> You are a Miserable Sham of AUTHORITY and RIGHTEOUSNESS

> Therefore; you are HEREBY, Impeached

In THIS BLESSED HOUR, and Upon THIS BLESSED DAY, in which you receive THIS DECLARATION:

> YOUR SUGGESTIONS OF FEAR AND VIOLENCE TOWARD THE PEOPLE OF GOD, SHALL BE MADE NULL AND VOID.

SINCERELY
THE PEOPLE OF GOD

Lightning Bug #28

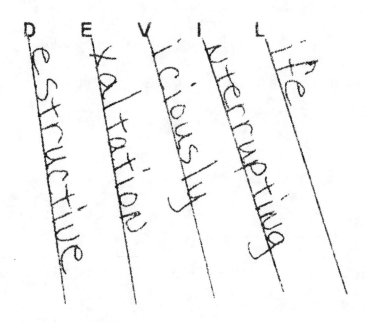

D E V I L

deStructive
EXaltation
vicious|y
interrupting
life

IT'S NO SECRET

JESUS has a "Witness Protection Program" that is available for:

> "Whom So Ever Will – Come, Believe, Confess, Repent, and be Baptized In the name of Jesus Shall be Saved from Spiritual death by Grace."

God will Forgive your Sins, and you will Miraculously become a new creature in Christ; whereby, you will be given a 'New Identity."

Your "New Name" shall be called:

> The "Son" or the "Daughter" of God

You will be "Relocated" (for your own protection) from the wilderness to the House of God; and eventually, transported into Heaven, a.k.a., The Kingdom of God-

> Home of the "Original" Godfather; or as "We, who are already "Under the Blood," like to call Him –

> **The Master of Masters**

Lightning Bug #94

Repentance of sin is:

"Good" grief

PROJECT "VARIANCE"

Perhaps, the Earth is an "arena"
Of toil, strife, and grief

Where struggles ensue
To possess the pleasures
Of celebrated beliefs

It's the market-place of virtues
That are valued, sold, and bought

A place where embellishments, such as
"Power" and "Dignity" are sought

It might be a meeting ground
Where immediate needs are met

Where strict/intermittent rules
And regulations are set

Perhaps, it's an atmosphere where "reality"
Intermingle with "desire and fantasy"

Causing mass confusion
That sometimes precede permanent
Loss of sanity

Suppose the area is an incubator
Or, a purging unit for the cultivation of the "raw" soul

A temporary shelter
Like a "womb" or a "mold"

It could be a stage or a campground
Or, some kind of training apparatus

Whereby, the "truth" and the "meek"
Are intercepted by the "sleek"

Which is generally known as "bully"
With a "cloak-and-dagger" physique

Lightning Bug #87

A "Worth-While" venture
To engage into

Is the "Demolition of Corruption"
That dwell "Within" you

THANK YOU, THANK YOU, THANK YOU

Thank you, Lord, for the "Gift of Praise"
Glory to your name

Thank you for the "Peace" you give
Also for sunshine, snow, and rain

Thank you for your "Healing Power"
And for the stars that shine at night

Thank you for "Spiritual Transformation"
From the "Darkness" into the "Light"

Thank you for the "Air" we breathe
And for birds that sing a tune

Thank you, Lord, for "EVERYTHING"
May "Thy Kingdom Come On Earth Soon"

Lightning Bug #58

Go ahead!
Take the plunge. Admit the "Truth," and back-stroke your way into
the Lord's "Good Grace."

LIFE'S BILL

What a blunder or what a wonder
Did God have in mind

He created me with so many faults
Some say, "I'm not worth a dime"

I try my hardest with all my might
All day long and even at night

No matter what a new day brings
Life is never how it seems

I'll never be able to foot the bill
Of this world's expectancy

So why, oh why, dear Lord
I pray, "why don't they just let me be"

Sometimes I wilt as flowers do
From trying to live the dream

It's not my fault that flesh and bones
Will come apart at the seams

Lightning Bug #47

Behind every proud stance or expression lurks MANIPULATION in all of its glory.

A CRY FOR AID

Hear me
When I pray, dear Lord
Remember that I am imperfect
And that I am a quiet spirit

Fill me
Oh, Sacred One
With your Divine substance
Save my soul from the grasp of famine

Mend my broken heart
According to thy grace
So that my flesh will not precede my soul
In the hour of prayer

Gratify my thirst for righteousness
In Jesus' name
For, thou arth my provider
AMEN

Lightning Bug #48

When "Arrogance" speaks: "Prejudice" listens, then, goes about "perpetuating" the "theory."

IN GOD'S SHOES

Walk a mile in God's shoes
And feel the indignation
Of being the "genius" behind the scene
But, classified as only a "sensation"

Walk a mile in God's shoes
And cry the tears of regret
For shattered dreams and utter confusion
In return for doing your best

Walk a mile in God's shoes
And march the lonely trail
Of carrying the burden all by yourself
Without anyone wishing you well

Walk a mile in God's shoes
And, then, you'll understand
What it is to produce fertile ground
Only to have it yield you "sand"

Walk a mile in God's shoes
And you'll have offsprings to delight your heart
You'll feel a sadness deep inside you
After tragedy has torn you apart

Walk a mile in God's shoes
And know the agony of the struggle
It takes to protect a lifetime of work
From turning into mere "rubble"

Walk a mile in God's shoes
And cherish a love so sweet
Only to discover that the love of your life
Turns out to be a "cheat"

Walk a mile in God's shoes
And soon you'll feel the thrust
Of betrayal from the ones you love
When all you did was trust

Walk a mile in God's shoes
And you will endure the sorrow
Of all the years of ungratefulness
With each given tomorrow

Walk a mile in God's shoes
And soar into the shame
Of all the injustice and waywardness
You, now, have become the blame

Walk a mile in God's shoes
And feel the sting of rejection
No longer a popular nominee
Therefore, voted out of the election

Walk a mile in God's shoes
And become an obsolete
No one will desire your services again
Because their standards, you will not meet

Walk a mile in God's shoes
And battle with the adversary
You know not whench it comes your way
Causing frequency of "peace" to vary

Walk a mile in God's shoes
And no lambs will you be roasting
Because a crook has stolen all of your wealth
And is now relaxing, mocking, and boasting

Walk a mile in God's shoes
And you will become a debit

You'll be stripped of all your glory
While the imposter becomes a credit

Walk a mile in God's shoes
And a mystery will unfold
This message solely tracks a thief
Who is layered under his gold

Walk a mile in God's shoes
And compassion for Him will emerge
You, then, can truly be a friend
To the One called "The Living Word"

Lightning Bug #36

GET REAL!
Parents are people, too:
God has assigned them to be a guardian to you while you are flourishing
into your maturity. They are a loan from God, and He ask only that
you treat them with respect in return for His consideration.

AND THE WINNER IS

Jesus is our "Role Model" for life
God wants us all to know

Ask me how I know this fact
It's cause "The Bible tells me so"

No "EMMY" or, No "GRAMMY"
Can take the place of "His Throne"

No matter what you've perceived in life
Or, what television cameras have shown

No "Head-Dress," "Hair-Style," or "Tiara"
Can ever take the place

Of His "RIGHTEOUS CROWN AND GLORY"
That GOD has ORDAINED above ALL
The "Human Race"

Lightning Bug #41

When you stand "steadfast" in the "Word" of God, "attitude" will try to "dictate" to you and "intimidate" you by hissing -

"So, what's your point?"

Never-the-less; know in your heart that you actually have unlimited points, because the "Word" is sharper than any two-edged sword.

GOD CREATED MAN IN HIS OWN IMAGE

A man is exceedingly joyful when his son is born. His face lights up with a ray of gladness. He sounds a trumpet and celebrates for days. He adores and protects him, and places no one or anything above him. He feels in his heart that the creation of his son is the most precious miracle that has ever happened, or shall happen. He is over-whelmed with pride. He is in his highest glory; nothing can surpass this achievement. He cannot be moved. He hovers over his son. He nurtures, provides, and desires all good things for him. He hopes in his heart that his son will grow up to think and act just like him. He knows that his son is a "replica" of him – His Masterpiece. He is the love of his life, his joy unspeakable, and his excellence. Life has new meaning, and the mystery is no longer a mystery.

Blessed be the name of our Lord, Jesus Christ, forever - AMEN

Lightning Bug #17

The "awesomeness" of the moon and stars
Reign in GLORY with "no-holds-barred"

The "pristine" splender of the sun and the clouds
Are "sanctioned" powers, but not one is proud

SPIRITS OF LOVE

As I shuffle through the crowd each day
Sometimes I almost lose my way

It's hard to keep a one-track mind
With all the commotion most of the time

Sifting through the endless faces
Of people going to various places

Bewildered me with a slight sensation
Of disregard and alienation

Low in spirit, but high in hope
That a kindred spirit will soon approach

And lead me to safety in a loving coach

Lightning Bug #11

The mind and the body are dependent upon each other for survival and are in a "marriage." God is their soul-mate, and they are bound by "Harmonious" submissions of "Grace," "Caring," and "Sharing." If one becomes distracted from the beat; then, disagreements and battles for control will ensue, inevitably, causing injury or death to the whole "marital" structure.

AND THEY SHALL BE A WITNESS OF HIM

Stripped of all pride
And sat aside
For God's sacred glory

Has left me with a burning desire
To tell you all this story

So, take the time
And lend an ear
To harken to the calling

Of what maybe a starting point
To prevent you, too
From falling

I used to be abrasive
Obnoxious, and uncaring

I prized myself on being provocative
And, no one could beat me "staring"

God must have been disgusted
Cause what He did was THIS

He took away my Earthly pride
Which abstracted me from the mix

He persistently chastised me
So as to evoke the respect
He was due

Resulting in this eruption of praise
SPEWING right out in front of you

Lightning Bug #80

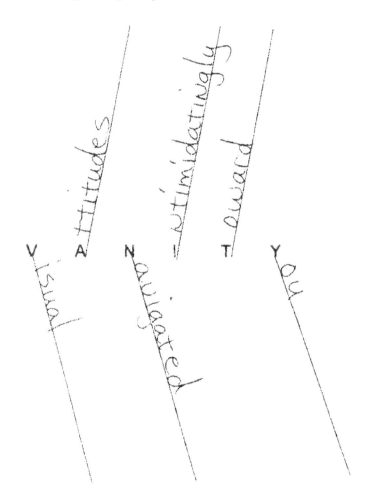

LISTEN

Heavenly hosts surrounds you
With mysteries unveiled

It's hard to know the truth sometimes
Because the world is full of tales

Look closely and listen carefully
To what God is constantly saying

The answer is always
And still the same

Never stop your "Praying"

Lightning Bug #8

BEWARE:

Fame is an extravagant prison that house the "wealthy," the "talented," and the "beautiful." The "Warden" is a subtle tyrant and thief that always solicit inmates with an elaborate proposal of prestige.

The longer the "Inmate's" occupancy, the higher are the chances that the "Inmate" will be robbed of "Vitality," "Privacy," and other "Priceless" virtues.

HAPPY HARVEST

Tarry not your labor unto the Lord
Lest, you lose your way

The "Road to Righteousness" is paved with "Blood"
Spilled by our Savior, JESUS CHRIST

Plant your seed
The harvest is near

For, God doesn't give us
The spirit of fear

Plant the "Good" seed
And soon you'll reap

A harvest of "Love"
Instead of deceit

Lightning Bug #59

The chemical combination of elements that create the "frictional" characteristics of the "force" called "sin" are:

1. excessive pride
2. excessive ambition
3. excessive jealousy
4. excessive competiveness
5. excessive anger
6. excessive rebellion

MORE GLORY

How awesome are thy
Power and Splender

You who command
Wind and sea to surrender

So Brilliant are your precept and way
I idolize you both night and day

Graced with Beauty so Radiant
No other can compete

Although, we often lie to ourselves
In our contemptible blind conceit

Oh, Soverign Lord
I humbly repent

Thou are a magnificent Wonder
Of Royal Descent

Lightning Bug #85

Constructive criticism and "tough" love can be positive "teaching" tactics only if they are "flanked" by "mercy" and 'understanding."

Without this "Endearment" or "Partnership," this form of discipline can only be perceived and looked upon as "cruel and unusual punishment."

DRESS ME, LORD

Sponsor my soul, Lord
If it be thy Will

I'm in need of a makerover
But, I can't afford the bill

What you see, Master
Is all that I am

You can see right through me
So, there isn't room for any source of a scam

I need a measure of courage
To Properly Represent YOU

There are aches in my body
And, I'm possibly tongue-tied, too

Size me up for a miracle fit
I don't want to sin anymore

Salvage the essence of thy heart's delight
And make me fashionably yours

Lightning Bug #84

Public Enemy #1:

ENVY

SHIFT TO THE RIGHT

Make a change for the better
Not for the worst

Let it be righteousness
That you thirst

Put down those weapons
And do not hate

Tell Jesus you want
To clean the slate

Shift your mind
To think "Good Thoughts"

Like the "Holy" god
Said that you ought

Be not fearful to make the change
And do not faint while trying

For, God is there to pick you up
And He hears you when you are crying

Don't worry about what your peers will think
Or, about what is whispered in the wind

Pleasing God is all that counts
Because that keeps you "FREE" from sin

Lightning Bug #63

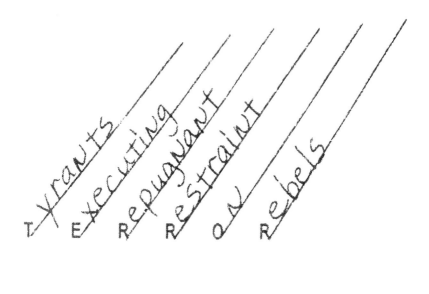

JUST CAUSE

It is an indignant jesture we convey when we conventionally claim calculated time and omnipotent independence from our Creator. God suffers from daily assaults, due to the false sense of wisdom subjective to mankind. We are not the "Genius;" but, are actually time-released collaborated portions of the Genius' cornucopia of Divine energy. When we insult God's creation, whether it be done self-righteously or inadvertently, we cannot omit offending God. It truly is relevant to question whether or not it is in the best interest of God for any society to believe that it is more honorable, classy, or efficient to surround their homes with well-kept flowers and shrubbery rather than provide a fruitful scenery of thriving young children sprouting about throughout the land.

Thank you, God, for your tolerance. Forgive us when we primp and flaunt our arrogance in the midst of your genius. In Jesus' name – AMEN

Lightning Bug #1

The stages of life for each entity are filmed, recorded, and stored for contemplation of redemption from the "Executive Producer of Life."

THE COURTSHIP

Is "Freedom" absolute, I say
Or, just a "word" that's often misconstrued

Evolutionized survival theories
Based solely upon individual mood

True, many have died, and many shall try
To possess the contents of it

But, none have penetrated the vault
That conceals this Distinguished "Nugget"

Lightning Bug #75

SELF-righteousness and SELF-preservation are fraternal twins; one is a male and the other is a female.

PILLARS

The "Awesomeness" and "Mystics" of "Childbirth" are relative to the "Clashing Turbulence of Thunder and Lightning," the "Trembling Effects of an Earthquake," the "Terrifying Trauma of an Eruption of a Volcano," and is "All Consuming;" but, be that as it may, BLESS GOD.

I believe that my "First" child taught me to "NOTICE and CARE" for someone other than myself.

I believe that my "Second" child taught me that the "WEAK and the FRAIL NEED PROTECTION."

I believe that my "Third" child (which was a miscarriage) taught me to "RESPECT LIFE before it is born;" because, you never know what the "Quality or Quantity" of INSPIRATION contained in the "PRECIOUS CARGO" being transported will REVEAL.

I believe that my "Fourth" child taught me to "HAVE COMPASSION, FEAR GOD, and to GIVE FROM THE HEART."

I believe that my "Fifth" child (which was a miscarriage) taught me to realize that, no matter how hard I try to stop mishaps from occurring, doesn't mean that I will always prevail. Sometimes, I just have to "LET GO" and "TRUST GOD."

I believe that my "Sixth" child taught me that when all seems hopeless, GOD WILL PREVAIL. Consequently; when I respond MERCIFULLY to the cries of the weak, I enable my own soul to "BE a BRIDGE to AID TOWARD the BETTERMENT of LIFE."

Lightning Bug #53

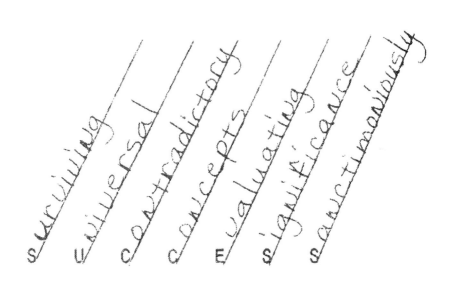

THE THINKER

The longer I think
I Should
I Might

The longer it takes me
To complete the flight

And when I think
I Can
I Shall

The Lord takes over
And all is well

I need the Lord
To guide my thoughts

Lest, my mind will think
What it not ought

Lightning Bug #35

Although, surprises are not always revealed and presented in a delightful fashion, and gifts are not always readily understood or appreciated; perhaps, the ability to receive the gift, is the most extraordinary gift within the gift.

THE CRY OF THE BABE

Nurture me, oh Lord
For, I am just a babe
And do not know the ways
Of your righteousness

Plant me in your bosom
So that I will feed from you

I have been poisoned and blinded
By the world around me

Purge me and cleanse my soul
To be fit for your Kingdom

For, I acknowledge your presence

Lightning Bug #61

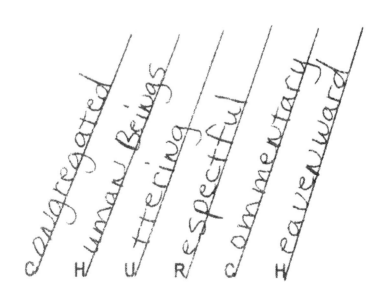

congregated
Human Beings
Uttering
Respectful
Commentary
Heavenward

THE JOURNEY

The stages of life and traveling
Are quite similar, it would seem

Mainly, because both MYSTIFY
And lead to fields and streams

BEHOLD, the Mountains and the Valleys
That occupy the Earth

The thunderous clouds and lightning bolts
Sent forth to quench its thirst

Inhale the air, and taste the food
That sprang up from the ground and trees

Our Creator deserves a "Standing Ovation"
Followed-up with our "Bended Knees"

Don't forget the Hills and Meadows
Nor, the inhabitants of the lands

The "Glory of God" is expressed throughout
The Ocean, the Sea, and the Sands

The awesomeness of the Galaxies
Are yet to be revealed

BEHOLD, another "Masterful Plan"
Pre-calculated and sealed

Although, life in the country
Maybe, contrary to life in the city

The sky above is always blue
And the "Sunset" is just as pretty

Don't forget the "Moon" and the "Stars"
That "Glorify" the night

Lord, life's journey is a stage
Of your "Phenomenal Creative Might"

Lightning Bug #16

CREATIVITY is thought provoking mental abstract; manifest in spirit, and absorbed by the sensory perception adrenaline flow of organic matter.

THE GLORIFIED BODY

This body of affliction and shame I wear
Is only for a season

For, God has a body prepared for me
That shall defy all human reason

So, if I seem a little worn
Or, scratched up from barbed-wire fence

It's because I've lived a rugged life
Struggling to survive all of life's suspense

Lightning Bug #12

Pardon me, Holy Spirit
But, would you "Hook-me-up"

With Absolute knowledge
Capabilities and trust

BEHOLD

A selfish heart and a hateful spirit
Shall be burned amongst the thistles

The thunderous might of "God's Angels of Wrath"
Will be resounding like a missile

Surrender now, ye evil-doers
For, God's Kingdom is at hand

Humble thyself before the Lord
His wrath cometh, and you shall not stand

Lightning Bug #23

The "blimp" must be the estranged, identical twin to the "ego" because:

1. They both flow "over-head"

2. They are both abnormally huge

3. They are both full of hot air

4. They are both always distracting others for the sole purpose of attracting "attention" to itself

THE LIGHT

There is a light that shines so bright
For everyone to see

Sometimes I think the storm won't pass
And that always frightens me

But, God's "Good Grace" embraces my soul
And turns my fear from new to old

I thank thee, Lord
For your Bright Light

That guides me through
Each morning and night

Lightning Bug #60

Should the creature invade his Creator's privacy by attempting to explore and possess the properties of His "pre-eminent" dimensional aura without first being granted a "sanctioned" invitation?

A CHAIN REACTION

The origin of bondage stems from a manipulative conception and venture pursued, enforced, and exercised by self-righteous psychopathic beings who ostracize others by haughtily assuming the status of God; whereby, wreaking havoc upon their subjects while frolicking betwixt nature in a fiendish, hot pursuit to possess wealth, immortality, and fame.

Lightning Bug #82

"Bathing flesh with exotic oils and soaps, and applying expensive perfumes and powders, does absolutely nothing to cover-up or cleanse away the blatant stench of deep-rooted sin." Thus, saith the Lord, Thy God.

RETRIEVED

I never believed in anyone
The way I believed in you

Until I discovered that the things you said
Were not exactly true

I visioned us eternally
Always being together

Sharing tender moments
Like birds of a feather

I thought you were my soul-mate
You seemed to understand

The sadness that I felt inside
And, you even held my hand

I turned against my parents
My family, and my friends

You became my everything
So, I thought that there was no end

You gave me hope and joy
No matter what the weather

I thought that no one on the face of this Earth
Could ever love me better

But, after all was said and done
And, time had taken its toll

You abandoned me to embrace another
And, you let my heart grow cold

I thank the Lord that all is well
PRAISE HIS HOLY NAME

If it wasn't for His intervention
I would be dead, or "Literally" insane

Lightning Bug #71

DIVISION

$$\text{Adultery} \overline{)\;\begin{array}{c} \underline{\text{Divorce}\ \ \text{r single}} \\ \text{M a r r i a g e} \\ \underline{-\,\text{S e p a r a t i o n}} \\ \text{r\ \ single} \end{array}}$$

59

REPORTING TO HEAD-QUARTERS

Dear Creator:

How are you? Fine I hope.

Just thought I would stop and take the time to write to you to tell you how I'm holding out on the Christian battlefield of life. I guess I'm doing o.k., considering the general infirmities of humanity and the sneak attacks of the enemy that come in season. What do you think? Some of the battles are more intense than others. I can't deny that I, myself, have suffered quite a few battle scars. Some you can visibly see, others you cannot. All-in-all, it is only by your grace, I remain. As you know, situations can become a bit weary. I am ashame to say, however, that I have become distracted and discouraged at times, and have fallen from grace. To tell you the truth, "sometimes I can barely muster enough faith to rise in the morning." I know these must be dishonorable or shameful words coming from a soldier on the battlefield; but, I'm just trying to keep it real. If I can't tell you, who else can I trust to tell? I know that my secrets are safe with you because, through it all, you have always been there for me. I know I haven't always appreciated you or given you your proper respect. I guess, what I'm really trying to say is, "thanks for everything, and forgive me for my shortcomings." I also would like to say that, "I think that you are the best listener that I have ever been blessed to communicate with. It is truly a priviledge to have you to confide in, in times such as these." I don't want to sound like a pessimist or anything; but, after-all, one never knows which battle will be his or her last. So, I have taken the liberty of making a list of some of the enemies that have sought to do me harm in the past:

1. Flattery
2. Thieves
3. Prejudice
4. Bullies
5. Disease
6. Envy
7. Diabolical Liars

8. Aggrogance
9. Selfishness
10. Hate

Needless to say, there are others who chose to operate in a more subtle manner, and those who preferred to attack incognito.

Please keep this list in your possession for safe-keeping as evidence of the perpetrators, in light of justice being served to the quilty conspirators in accordance to your Grace, Mercy, and Power.

Well, I guess I'll close for now.

Hope to hear from you soon.

Yours truly,
Christian Soldier of Life

Lightning Bug #105

Don't stay stuck in the mud. Stop "Spinning Your Wheels," and let Jesus be your "Back-up Plan."

SUPER GOD

Find "PEACE" with God
And soon you'll see

What life is truly
Meant to be

Tell Him your fears
And all your troubles

For, He knows how to sort
Through all the rubble

There's nothing too big
For Him to tackle

Because, His hands are not tied
And His Feet are not shackled

He'll put things in perspective
So neat, and oh, so tighty

Because, He is the "One and Only"
GOD ALMIGHTY

Lightning Bug #42

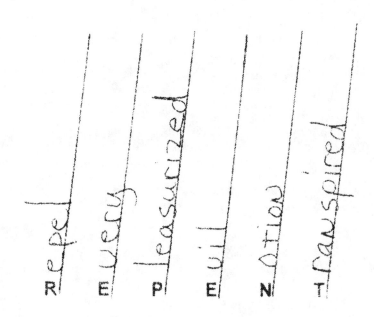

repel
very
pleasured
uit
ation
transpired

R E P E N T

THE BORDER

Jesus lives inside of me
So, my heart bears a sign that reads
"No Vacancy"

With bolted locks to prevent home invasion
My soul is secure from enemy persuasion

Praise God
My tormented soul is free
To dance and sing the victory

Lightning Bug #3

FLAMBOYANCY is nothing more than an extreme "twist" of the "ordinary" gone "array."

WE LOVE YOU, FATHER

FATHER/GOD, the SON, the HOLY GHOST

We're here to Bless your name forever
From "Coast to Coast"

Because, you're "Righteous and Just"
To all of us

We know in our hearts
It's you we can "TRUST"

Thank you, Father, for Jesus
The "Sacrificial One"

No one else can do
What He has already done

"REDEEMING" our SOULS
With His "Precious Blood"

Is truly an act
Of unselfish love

Because the price was paid
And it cost Him His life

We Bless His name
And REPENT of all strife

Thank you, Father
For welcoming all of us back

With "Mansions" for homes
Instead of old shacks

HALLELUJAH! to you, Father
May you "Reign in Glory"

And Bless the entire world over
To receive the "Virgin Mary/Jesus" story

Lightning Bug #37

Humble ground is "Sacred" ground.

A PLEA FOR MERCY

Oh, Precious Lord

Is there no escape
From my ignorance
My dereliction
Or, my insorbordination

Spare me from the scope of your disappointment
And the scepter of your vengeance
For, I am your fragile servant
In constant need of your guidance and stability

Bless me
Have mercy on me
My soul yearns
For your approval

AMEN

Lightning Bug #21

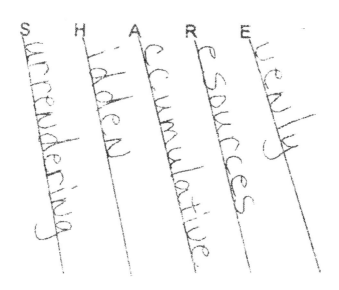

S H A R E evenly
surrendering laden accumulative resources

REALISM

Reality is to me, you see
God revealed it to me so

It's He who causes me to live
Stop basking in His "GLO"

I was so twisted with conceit
I worshipped myself from head to feet

I could not see the Light at all
And knew not the ways of God

Till Jesus saved my wretched soul
From Satan, who was trying to rob

The struggle within to be free from sin
Is near its ending time

"Peace be Still," Jesus said to me
For, don't you realize you're mine

Lightning Bug #92

Why is "History" prone to repeat itself?

Answer: Because "History" is a form of immortality, and it's re "psych"able.

I AM

I've been pre-selected
To be neglected
Rejected, and disrespected –
     Who Am I

I've been pursued, misconstrued
Purposely confused, and morbidly reproved –
     Who Am I

I've been bombarded, suffocatingly guarded
Systematically sorted
And labeled "retarded"
Then, perceived as "out-smarted" –
     Who Am I

I've been lured
Venomously smeared
Publicly sneered
And editorially jeered –
     Who Am I

I've been critically acclaimed
As being the one that is "lame"
Obviously, "insane"
Thus, tailor-made for a derogatory name –
     Who Am I

I've been falsely accused of crimes
Wounded multiple times
Smothered and doused with lime –
     Who Am I

I've came eye to eye with fear
And have been known to have shed a tear
But, still I persevere

For, I am the bona fide spirit
Called "Freedom"
Sanctioned by the Creator
    I AM ETERNAL

LET FREEDOM RING

*This poem is dedicated to Dr. Martin Luther King, Jr., Andrew
Goodman, James Earl Chaney, Michael Henry Schwerner,
Viola Liuzzo, and all others who have unjustly lost their lives
for the sake of God defending freedom and justice for others.*

Lightning Bug #56

Life is a constant array of diversified monolithic hypocrisies, embedded in an atmosphere marked by sacrifice, in the essence of deceit for the sake of ambition.

THE GRAIN OF MUSTARD SEED

God has planted His Church in me
To tower over shrubs so the world can see

A Sanctified, Holy
God-Fearing tree

His Blood washed me so pure and clean
That I am no longer "selfish and mean"

My branches will yield leaves
Of "love and devotion"

To help others needing help
To calm the storm of their emotions

The fruit I will bear
Will be "Heavenly Blessed"

Because, God has ordained me
To do my best

To "Glorify" my Father, "UP ABOVE"
I give full Honor to my One True Love

When the "Harvest" is ripe
It shall be so sweet

And, I'll humbly place it
At my "MASTER'S" feet

Lightning Bug #91

The "Church" is not a "fashion show" or club. It is a "shelter," a "hospital," and a "rehab" for spiritually twisted souls to experience exorcism and recuperation; so that they can be accepted and reunited with the author and finisher of their faith.

ROCK-A-BYE

If one loses his virtue to Flattery
That one has, unfortunately, been "DUPED"

Because Flattery is an instigator
Who likes to roam around and snoop

Attempting to defile hearts that are "prep" for Glory
A TRAIT that is found exclusively in the roots

But, be of Good Cheer
Jesus is the cure

To purify and make whole
God's children

Put to rest all FEARS
He's the "Gentle Savior"

VERY THOROUGH
So, He never forgets to wash behind the ears

Children need to be taught the truth
Not grow up trusting in fables

Cause, Flattery takes pleasure
At "Virtue's" expense

When it is able to rob the cradle

Lightning Bug #13

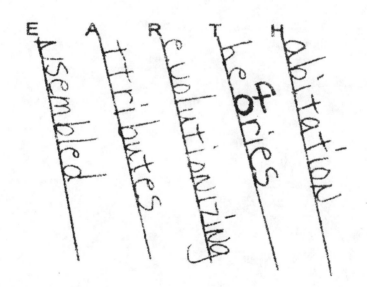

E — dissembled
A — ttributes
R — evolutionizing
T — heories
H — abitation

DIVIDED WE STAND

One side of me is weak
The other side is strong

One side of me does what is right
The other side does what is wrong

One side of me is life
The other side is death

One side of me cares for others
The other side cares for self

One side of me is meek
The other side is prudent

One side of me is a "know-it-all"
The other side is a "student"

One side of me is serious
The other side is folly

One side of me is sadness
The other side is jolly

One side of me is new
The other side is old

One side of me is a melting pot
The other side is a mold

One side of me is private
The other side is alluring

One side of me is insecure
The other side is reassuring

One side of me is visual
The other side is reclusive

One side of me is "matter-of-fact"
The other side is "illusive"

One side of me will surely die
The other side will linger

One side of me will turn into dust
The other side will turn into a singer

God has fashioned me as such
For, thus, the "story" is told

One side of me is "Flesh," you see
But, the other side is soul

Lightning Bug #50

The "Holy Spirit" is a "disciplinary" for out-of-control, unrepentant spirits.

AWE

You amaze me, Lord
The things you do

With virtue so pure
And "WORD" that "REMAINS" true

No longer will I view the world
The way I used to see it

It's you I desire above all else
Because, your "Love" has taken precedence

Who can deny your "Power"
Your "Charity" and your "Wit"

I "Adore" you, Holy Spirit
Because you "Saved Me from the Pit"

Lightning Bug #25

Isn't it "Ironic" that some of us are so pampered and presumptuous, that we spend a lifetime being happy and proud to be able to "raise hell;" then, when death appears to be inevitable, all we want, then, is to be "Rewarded" by being granted the ability to "Rest-in-Peace."

TIME

Many years have passed away
And my mind begins to wonder

What happened to the tender years
Of childhood, fun, and blunder

Time is not forever
Each day we have is blessed

Love someone other than yourself today
And God will do the rest

Lightning Bug #34

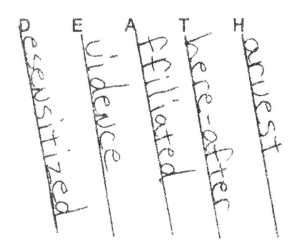

ALL HAIL THE KING OF KINGS

Believe in Jesus
The Son of God

The One who rules
With an "Iron Rod"

There is no other
Nor, shall there ever be

A king throughout the nations
To match his Divinity

Stop deceiving yourselves
Claiming all reason

Don't you know
You'll reign for only a few seasons

The battle for the Kingdom
Was already won

The night Christ Jesus
Was blessedly born

Lightning Bug #9

What do you get when you cross a mirror with an "Ego?"

Answer: A MIRAGE

THE MANY ROLES OF LIFE

The dramatics of life
Have taken their toll

As tales of truth
And myths unfold

Ancient lyrics and relics retrieved
Alter thoughts of what is perceived

The secret passage to curios reveal
Death-bed wishes buried and sealed

When will enough, be enough
And why must the heart still crave

The lure of success is an illusive game
Of simply "robbing graves"

Lightning Bug #18

If authenticity and value are designated by vintage; then, shouldn't "God" be considered to be invaluable and "Much-To-Be-Desired?"

FOREVER PRAISING

My soul cried out to God
And, He consoled me
For, He is a Forgiving
And Inspiring Mentor

Worship belongeth to you, oh Lord
It is a privilege to do your Will
Compassion generates from you
You are the Omnipotent Preserver of Energies

When I Falter
You sustain me
Oh, Lord of understanding
Patience abideth with you

You are a Lighthouse
A breath of fresh air
The dolphin that carries me safely to shore
And, the SEAL that consecrate my soul

Blessed be the Rock
Of the Holy Foundation
Forever and Ever
AMEN

Lightning Bug #14

Maybe, the "Blueprints" to living in this world are liken unto a "maze" or a cross-word puzzle; because, we always seem to be driven to "Get-In-Where-We-Fit-In," before we can acquire the dividend.

DOVES

Peaceful creatures of the world
Are there for God's good glory

Pay attention to what their lives portray
They "simply" tell a story

Peaceful sounds of inspiration
Fills your heart with laughter

A joyful noise unto the Lord
Today and FOR-EVER-AFTER

Lightning Bug #29

Those who place full credence IN and base their social attitudes ON the synopsis, "Blood is Thicker than Water," will consequently, soon end up "Dangerously Dehydrated."

THE MASK

The mask I wear
Is just a sham

Of who I really
And truly am

I'm merely a child
Who never grew up

Surrounded my sin
And misery and such

Lost and confused
About what was right

I could hardly ever
Rest at night

As years go by
I seek a new route

God, grant me the "Wisdom"
To figure it all out

Lightning Bug #7

Born a sinner
Redeemed by Christ

Much love to the SAVIOR
For His Sacrifice

POWER TO THE HOLY SPIRIT

HALLELUJAH!
Welcome, Holy Spirit
Blessed be thy Formation

May Power, Righteousness, and Justice
Be thy Crown, thy Throne, and thy Pedestal
Eternally

Possess my soul, Lord
I pray
If it be thy Will
For, I am at your disposal

Let the Young and the Aged
Bring forth acceptable praise
Peace unto you

Thank you
May thy WILL be honored
Forevermore
               AMEN

Lightning Bug #5

Don't invest too much of your common "cents" in your "perky" youthfulness, or "stunning" beauty; because, you just might end up disappointingly bankrupt, with nothing in your bank account or "trust" fund, but a wrinkled bag full of old dry bones.

SECURITY

Security be a friend of mine
Abide with me throughout the times

Place me up on solid ground
And let not "fear" pull me down

Level the bold aggression
Dispensed to me with grief

Leave not a trace of that "anxious" spirit
Called "The Agony of Defeat"

Let me enjoy the "Goodness"
That "virtue" has to offer

Soothe the harshness of the world
By making "hearts" a bit more softer

Lightning Bug #57

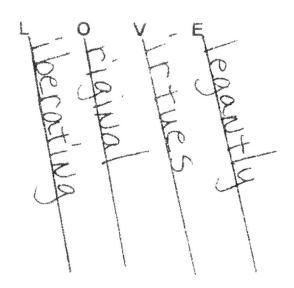

THE GRACE PERIOD

Although days turn into years
Sometimes with "Frustration" and tears

You must remember
That God's "Rapture" nears

Be strong in "Faith"
Hold on tight

Pray all day and into the night
That God will bring all things to light

In time your sorrow
Will melt away

And you'll "Thank the Lord"
For His "Blessed" day

Lightning Bug #67

Maybe, one cannot truly rid one's self totally of life's stressful situations; but, when you can trade or eliminate the negative to embrace the positive, you lay a new foundation for a more fertile lifestyle.

MYSTIC HAUNTINGS

We are all just strangers
In this foreign land

Wandering to and fro each day
Needing a helping hand

Misplaced and disconnected
From ancestral rites-of-culture

Has created a sense of alienation
Mingled with mental torture

I do not desire to beg of you
Or, steal from you and yours

I only await for "The Keeper of Souls"
To open up Freedom's doors

I know He sees this degradation
And tribulations that come in season

For, He alone will right the wrongs
Unjustified in reason

Troubled souls beseech you, Lord
To take hold of feeble hands

And guide us through your passage way
That leads to Freedom land

Use your key of mercy
To set the captives free

And let the nations stand in "AWE"
Of your "Masterful Artistry"

Bind the evil spirits
Whose powers are competition and hate

And grant unto us your peace and tranquility
According to your grace

Strike down the spirit of selfishness
Which leads to utter destruction

Disguised under the names familiarly called
"Prosperity" and "Production"

Lightning Bug #45

What do you get when you mix "Sensuality" with "Holiness?"

CHURCH

God is the OWNER and Chief Engineer of Souls. He holds in His possession, the maintenance criteria and mold pertaining to one and all to substantiate His claim. Our bodies are the Temporary Temples that He has chosen for His Holy Spirit to reside in. The bodies are utilized, somewhat, like incubators or greenhouses, while God nurtures, instruct, and reshape the Spirit into its maturity; for His Purpose and Glory.

Jesus is the CEO of the Soul Patrol authorized to supervise, repair, and prepare the sanctioned TEMPLES by evicting all Unclean spirits and removing the hazardous waste, THEREIN, associated with sin.

Lightning Bug #110

Those who are longing
To transcend to a more positive side

Must first resolve
How to swallow their Earthly pride

THE DISH

Bitter-sweet memories of childhood
Ponder in the minds of many

Hardship and strife deep within
Comes glooming through
The eyes of men

Tears and laughter
Mixed together
Sunshine, rain, snow
Whatever

Mixed up well and served with venom
Is nature's appetizer for life
That we all are given

Brutality and hate
Ice cream and cake
Thus
Appears to be an unhealthy plate

Lightning Bug #20

Playing chess with God is a "No Brainer."

LORD, DON'T FORGET

Lord, don't forget I'm fragile
And too weak to behold your "Glory"

Don't forget your mercies, Lord
For those who believed the story

I battle with myself each day
To walk the straight and narrow

Direct me when I go astray
Just like you do the sparrow

Lightning Bug #51

Precede with tackful progress, and recede hypocrisies leading to unjust.

Direct Credit and Insurance Policy Application
for the "soul" purpose of forming
an allegiance with God
(for the "Betterment" of life)

This insurance coverage is available to whom-so-ever will, by faith, heed to the beckoning demeanor of a Justified, Devout, Sacrifical Savior and Shepherd of the lost and redeemed: THE LORD, JESUS CHRIST, THE SON OF GOD

Check (√) here to see if you qualify for redemption

	Yes	No
1. Are you willing to take initiative and began conducting frequent and somewhat extensive soul-searching meditational sessions to reflect upon your true ambitions, skills, and fidelities bequeath to you by the current said guarantor of gratuities of your said status?	☐	☐
2. Are you willing to denounce/repudiate all association with your present "bogus" soul insurance policy holder?	☐	☐
3. Are you willing to submit to the Lord by giving your permission to receive treatment from God based upon a physician/patient level of intimacy?	☐	☐

*If your answer is "yes" to this question, please read carefully:

Some purging of the soul is needed, and will be performed on all applicants, pending "Just Cause."

*NOTE: There maybe some irritation and queasiness following purging.

4. Are you spiritually bankrupt now?
   *Any experience in the area of spiritual
   bankruptcy is a plus.

       ☐   ☐

   Hence: Applicants must be exceptionally
   FLEXIBLE i.e., liken unto clay
   in the hands of a supreme potter.

5. Are you willing to coward down in the sight of
   the Lord, and beseech mercy and forgiveness? ☐ ☐

6. Are you willing to relinquish your Earthly pride? ☐ ☐

7. Are you willing to shed the skin of worldly sensuality? ☐ ☐

8. Are you willing to open your mind to
   changes that are geared toward and
   pursuant to the betterment of life, by
   leaning not toward humanistic reasoning or
   understanding; but, rather, trust in the Lord
   with all your heart, mind, and soul, and love
   your neighbor as you do yourself? ☐ ☐

9. Are you willing to be completely submerged
   under water, and be baptized in the name of
   "Jesus" for the remission of sin? ☐ ☐

10. Check list before signing application:

    *Only serious applicants need apply

    a. Spiritually bankrupt? ☐ ☐

b. Soul experiencing an over-whelming urge to embrace Christ? ☐ ☐

c. Applying with an open mind and a free will? ☐ ☐

☐ ☐

d. Did you leave your "ego" out of this application?

——————————————
Applicant's Signature

(Date) ——————————
Year of Our Lord Jesus Christ

Lightning Bug #90

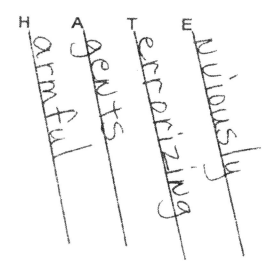

THE DILIGENT SOWER

The "Gifts" of FAITH and PATIENCE
Are "Sacred" treasures, "You Should Know"

So, take heed, ye laborers, and never give up
Although, the "REAPING" maybe slow

Tend to the SEED
And shield it from drought

"FAITHFULLY" pray over it
And do not doubt

"PRAISE" the Lord
With all your might

"BLESS" His HOLINESS
For, this is RIGHT

Lightning Bug #10

A boat in the water
Will, most definitely, get rocked
With rhythmic waves
After leaving the dock

Thus, the boat on the land
Shall assume the position
Of a harbored vessel
Awaiting a Captain's rendition

MY HERO

My soul is wounded deeply
What a story it has to tell

But, God knows all my secrets
And He will make me well

Emotionally crippled from deception and sin
Sends my world into an awful spin

Filled with grief
And heartaches to bear

It seems like all I can do
Is sit and stare

Drowning in sorrow
And fatigue from all the "chatter"

God keeps quiet
For, He knows what is the matter

And when my soul has weakened
From all the stress of life

God is there to rescue me
And gives me the strength to fight

Lightning Bug #22

Stress and life
Go hand-in-hand

In conjunction with the "desires"
And the "needs" of "Mortal" man

BLESS HIM

My Lord has taken me
From ashes to Glory
Bless His Holy name

From bitterness
To Gladness
Praise His Holy name

For, the light of God
Is in me
Because He delivered me
Out of darkness

Bless His Holy Name
For, He is Good

He has shone His Light
In the secret dark places
Of my soul
Now, there is light

Praise His Holy name
For, He is Great

Where there was coldness
Now, there is warmth

Bless His Holy name
For, He is God

Lightning Bug #32

No "one" is indispensable, except "God."

DELIVER ME

Direct my ways, Lord
Both day and night

Shine on me
With your Heavenly Light

Singe my soul
With urging desire

To do your will
With Holy Ghost Fire

Fix my wings
So I can fly

Safely to you
And tell the world, "Goodbye"

Lightning Bug #49

Get your house in order
By ridding it of all poison sumac

That bind and twist the heart strings
Which hinder "true love" from making a come-back

THE GIFT OF LOVE

God in His infinite wisdom
Has blessed me with this gift

To love my neighbor as I do myself
And sow seeds to spiritually lift

I'll bless Him in the morning
In the evening, and at night

I'll love all creatures, both big and small
For, God said, "This is Right"

Lightning Bug #40

Oftentimes, the price of highly sought after, desired liberties such as: Happiness, Health, and Pleasures are paid for with abstract substances called Blood, Sweat, Tears, and Agony of exposed vulnerability and humility, scrutinized and sacrificed peremptorily, without the benefit of mercy.

I SHALL PREVAIL

Jesus loves me
And He knows

That I am "Merely"
A "Mortal" soul

Jesus loves me
Cause He said

He'll be my Shelter
And my "Bread"

In His "Blood"
I'm enveloped within

To cleanse me of
My "Fleshly" sin

Through the tears and aniexty
I fight to win the bout

To "FREE" my mind
Of "prejudice," "self-righteousness," and "doubt"

And when my numbered days have ceased
I'll finally be able to "REST in PEACE"

No more aches and pain to bear
Just Jesus' embrace, and God's tender care

Lightning Bug #95

Prejudice, greed, cruelty, and hate are precious, "To-Die-For," heirlooms to some of us.

WITH ALL DUE RESPECT

What can I say, or what can I do to mend your heart of the wounds of neglect and dishonor I have displayed unto you, oh, Lord? For, surely, I was wrong in my ways and my thinking. You are all things that are good and pure. You are too good for me, Lord. I do not deserve all the goodness you give unto my ungrateful and disobedient spirit; yet, you sustain me in your good grace. Great are you, because you are clothed in mercy and love for all that move in the Earth. You are beautiful, unique, and divine in every way. You are a life-giving formula of radiant light, girded in omnipotent power and righteousness. Your eyes are stones of love, and your mouth is a great fountain that spew out Heavenly truths and revelations. Your breath is a life-giving force. Without you, there is no life. Love and righteousness are your weapons of choice, and your "Word" is sharper than any two -edged sword. Your body secretes Holy oils, which are healing agents and a sweet smelling savor.

Lightning Bug #69

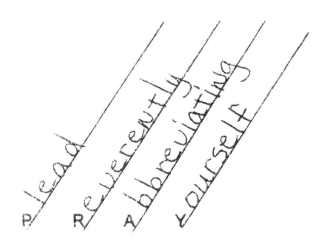

P Plead

R Reverently

A Abbreviating

Y Yourself

SO MUCH, SO LITTLE

So much work
So little time

So many tears
So many are mine

So much pride
So little care

So much self-righteousness
So many in despair

So much grief
So much pain

So little comfort
So much shame

So little construction
So much destruction

So much hate
So little love

I cry out to thee
My God above

Lightning Bug #96

Behold:

Criticism is a "Spiritual Brush" used to "Buff," or sometimes "Erase," mental activity from the 'Blueprint of Productivity."

GLOAT-TICIANS

Brag-racing is a "Popular" sport
For those who waddle in pride

Reminiscing about "Chaotic" events
While basking in the vibes

They set the pace
With a smiling face

As they lead others to believe
That they are the "Greatest"

And, surely, within their rights
To do whatever it takes to succeed

Away they go to "Celebrate"
The victories of their "Actions"

With "Chuckling" hearts that "Lavishly" yield
Irreversible "Premeditated" Fractions

Lightning Bug #44

Hate is a contaminated, contagious Earthly yolk of secretion, caused by digesting and retaining large quanities of composed hypocriscy, combined with profused injections of spiritual concentration of vanity.

GOD, A.K.A., LOVE

Love is a most tender and precious gift; so delicate and fragile, so gentle to the touch, so adorable. It is a phenomenal existence of Heavenly Powers of Goodness waiting to be absorbed and consumed into weak vessels to heal and restore. It is an odyssey to be treasured and secured with all diligence and respect that one can induce one's soul to substantiate. It is a warm life-giving force to all living things, waiting to saturate the Earth and all of its inhabitance, to nourish and replenish it. It is a rich oozing of "Divine Aura" waiting to circulate throughout the nations. It is a rare sacred relic of pure power and might that cannot be replaced or shut off: For, to do so, would forge the prelude of a devastating ending.

BLESSED BE THE HOLY ONE

Lightning Bug #2

The "objective" is to succeed

Without offending "God"
Or harboring greed

While helping others
That also have needs

HELP

Embrace me, Lord
For, I am weak

Teach me how
To walk and speak

Bestow unto me
Your loving grace

And bring a smile
Onto my face

Wash me in
Your "Blood of Life"

For, you alone
Have paid the price

Catch me when
I fall from grace

And sat me in
My proper place

Cherish me with
A love so true

That makes me
Want to "worship" you

Place me up
On solid ground

And forever remind me
That you're always around

Equip me with
The tools I need

To plow through trials
And plant good seed

Prepare the ground
And make it fertile

So that the fruit will multiply
And be not sterile

Lightning Bug #27

The "Lust Factor," which is Based upon "desire," COMPOUNDED with "pretense," DIVIDED by "endurance," MULTIPLIED by "resource," is EQUAL to the Sum of "gratification," MINUS the "consequence."

KING JESUS

Hundreds of tears of inspiration
Have fallen from my eyes

Ever since my soul was saved
From that hateful "Father of Lies"

I live to tell the rest of you
Who doubt the Savior's Power

He hears you in the crowded places
And even in the shower

Talk to Him, "one-on-one"
Tell Him you need repentance

He'll send His Holy Spirit right down
To help His renowned descendant

Lightning Bug #4

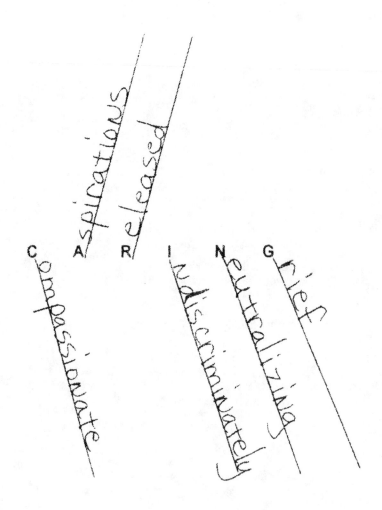

CARING
- aspirations
- released
- compassionate
- indiscriminately
- neutralizing
- grief

THE RIDE

When I was "LOST"
I did believe that I was "invincible"

My "alter" ego told me, too
That I was "indispensable"

The "party-life" had stolen my heart
And had taken it on a "joy-ride"

I concentrated on my "outer appearance"
But, neglected my soul that lived on the inside

"Common Sense" took a back seat
While "Folly" rode up front

Never caring about who got hurt
We commenced to plow over all the speed bumps

Full of "Fancy," and full of "Self"
The competition was ON

To burn rubber around all travelers
Who were cruising in my zone

The ride was "intoxicating"
And "dashing," to say the least

My "virtue" had begun to "run-a-muck"
While never appearing to cease

Driving with the "high beams"
Turned on at all times

Has a "blinding" affect
Upon the natural "human mind"

The road was "loaded" with turns
Which ended in a "surprising" twist

With "Jesus" towing
My soul back home

At the "Cross-Road"
Opposite the pit

Lightning Bug #43

CAUTION:

Don't confuse the "tranquility" that surrounds "simplicity" with boredom.

FOREVER GRATEFUL

Thank you, Lord
For this gift of praise

To help me through
These trying days

Thank you for the love you give
Which teaches us all how we ought to live

Thank you for the air we breathe
And for the food you supply each day

Thank you for your presence, Lord
And for hearing us when we pray

Thank you, God, for Jesus
Who died to save the world

Thank you for my baby boy
And for my baby girl

Thank you for your "Staying" power
And for mercies in abundance

Thank you, God, for creating us
You keep us forever "astonished"

Lightning Bug #52

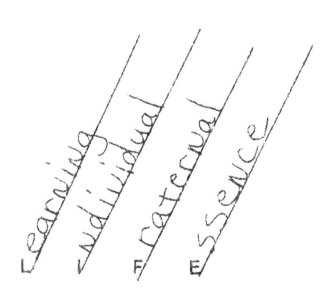

TREASURE TROVE

To be at peace with God
And one's self

Is more valuable Than
All the riches of the world

More precious Than
Diamonds or pearls

More sacred Than
Gold, or rubies by the truck load

Lightning Bug #19

Position Wanted

Washed-up sinner seeks rehabilitation and power from God, the Creator of all things. Would be willing to sacrifice my "pride" and my "arrogance" in return for "mercy" and "forgiveness."

UNDER GOD'S PROTECTION

Angel wings shield me
From the storms that lie ahead

Protect me from the nightmares and such
That disturb me in my bed

Trumpet sounds surround me
And birds sing a lovely tune

Angels prepare a meal for me
That I will be enjoying soon

I know the Lord will comfort me
Whenever I fall or stumble

He braces me with tender mercies
And keeps me Steadfast and Humble

Lightning Bug #15

VIRTUE - Flattery's claim to "Fame"

HALT! WHO GOES THERE

It has come to the attention of the Soul Patrol Council that there are a questionable amount of Born Again children of God who are haphazardly participating in "competitive praise and testimony" sessions. They are those who are so competitive that they intermittently use their God-given Gifts and Blessings to insinuate "favoritism." Haughtily exalting their own "presumably" HIGHER status with God than the other blood-washed children. Thus, attributing to the ever present "festering" of jealousy and sibling rivalry that exist in those who are yet "carnal." Be assured that such displays and claims do not go undetected. They are unwarranted, and counter-productive to the Kingdom of God. Know also that God's love is Timeless, Plentiful, and Unnatural; unlike that of the world's. Therefore, it is CERTIFIABLY INCOMPREHENSIBLE. God is able to love and maintain all. His WORD is BOND. This behavior is inappropriate and unhealthy for the Church. In the world, you respect each other and retrieve honor from your, said, bloodline; but, ALL in the FAMILY of God SHALL retain honor from the "Blood" and the "WATER."

Lightning Bug #86

I GET A THRILL WHEN I'M DOING GOD'S WILL.

AN ABUNDANCE

Born a mystery
Life begins

Knowing not its purpose
Nor, fearing its end

At first it appears
From an awkward glance

That Life has taken
A formal stance

A source of energy
To be cherished

Has seized the moment
To be nourished

A lifetime of hunger
And a lifetime of thirst

Are lifetime conditions
That come with the birth

Born dependent
From birth, it seems

Make living for some
A burdensome thing

If Life was not enveloped
Betwixt the selfish and the greedy

Then, Life would become a bit more able
Instead of being so needy

Lightning Bug #62

To think more highly of oneself than one ought to, is a congestive state of mental stability, due to the "malignant" growth of an "egotistic" head-stone.

MY PASSION

My passion for the Lord
Is like no other

My heart does a dance
Like the butterfly's flutter

Because He's sweet
And kind to me

I often feel like
The honeybee

Drawn to Him
To do His will

Stuck like glue
To His Haven on the hill

Lightning Bug #31

The spirit can't be "humbled"
Until the "flesh" is crumbled

SYMPHONY

Strive to regard, promote, and to heal
Try not to envy, destroy, or to steal

Creative "Flavor" is phenomenal
It intrigues the senses and is not abomiable

Savor the aroma of this artistic over-tone
Urging the willing to right the wrong

You have it within your capacity to achieve
The utmost reward of greatness, indeed

An ill-willed heart, gathers nothing more
Than ill-gotten gain from envy's door

Lightning Bug #83

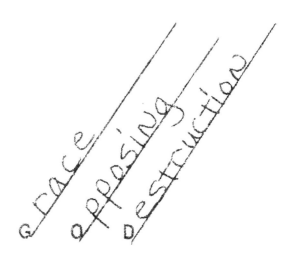

TRIFLING

The CHURCH
Is OBLIGED
To REPRESENT God
What a tremendous RESPONSIBILITY

But, Lord bear with me
I want to serve you right
Please, DON'T consider
Getting rid of me

It's not that
I don't want to please you
Contrarily
I crave to do your Will

PATHETICALLY
My "flesh" isn't shatter-proof
And, it TENDS to indulge
In TOO many WORLDLY FRILLS

Lightning Bug #109

There are 2 notorious thieves that should be featured on "America's Most Wanted." Robbing individuals and families of their "sanity" and "good fortune" faster than a frog can catch a fly is their M.O. They give new meaning to the phrase "Terrible 2's." Their names are "PREJUDICE" and "PRIDE." They should be considered to be "PRETENTIOUS" and "EXTREMELY DANGEROUS" to the development and rehabilitation of God's creation.

My Beloved Groom:

I miss you so much. My heart fails me of the words to express my loneliness. I know that one glance from you will melt the icicles of loneliness inside my soul. Thank you for sending Jesus to comfort me here; that was very thoughtful of you. Without Him, life would have been even more unbearable. My passion for you is like no other. I am like a child at Christmas time unwrapping presents. My heart aches with anticipation of your arrival and our wedding. I cannot tell you how many sleepless nights I've spent thinking of you since you've been away. I yearn for your strong, yet so gentle, arms to embrace me; and for your soft lips to caress mine. I need to feel the warmth of your sweet breath in my ear whispering, "I Love You." You are everything to me. Without you, I am without life. There is no reason to live, because you are the meaning of life. I adore and worship you. You are my ultimate mate. I want our wedding to be so perfect. Everything has to be just right. I tremble as I prepare myself for you and this up-coming "GLORIOUS" event; and pray that you will find me to be tasteful and pleasing in thy sight. I hope I am the "Chaste" bride of your heart's delight.

Eternally,
Your Bride

Lightning Bug #24

The only "true" cure for a "contrite" heart is a dose of "compassion" from God.

Lightning Bug #33

Being "granted" mercy from our Creator is the "greatest" gift that God can bestow unto us. Pray for "MERCY."

INTENT

Those who maneuver their faculties
To wage war on the disabled and the meek

Will cause The Good Lord to SCORN
And the angels in Heaven to weep

Life contains a strange
Assortment of fate

So, cling on to JESUS
Because He's Greater than Great

The meaning of life
Is not ALL about pleasure

Nor, is it a constant joy
The WORK of God

Is SERIOUS business
GOD IS NOT A TOY

Lightning Bug #107

Don't worry!
God is not a "FAD."
He won't leave you hanging.

LOYALTY

Is the term, "loyalty," a.k.a., "give and take:"

(a) a "realistic" source of energy

(b) just "great expectations of hope," harbored in the heart as payment for debts or favoritism shown toward another

(c) a virtuous quality

(d) a manipulative tool used to control another "Being"

(e) a support factor

(f) a contract enter into, "verbally or written"

(g) an inherited benefit package

(h) a religious "rite-of-passage"

(i) the "KEY" that is used to open and lock the doors to "Good and Evil"

Lightning Bug #113

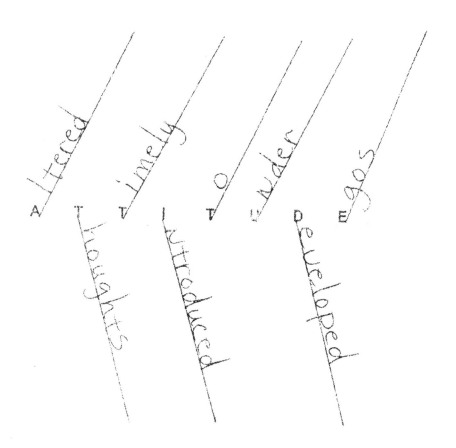

SEEDS

Somethings are good
And somethings are bad

Somethings make us happy
While other things make us sad

Somethings are true
And somethings are false

Somethings are gains
While other things are a loss

Somethings are given
And somethings are taken

Somethings are a "free-for-all"
While other things are forsaken

Somethings give us pleasure
And somethings give us pain

Somethings give us peace-of-mind
While other things drive us insane

Somethings are inspirational
And somethings are depressing

Somethings promote a healthy life
While other things are distressing

Somethings, undoubtedly, will set us free
And somethings will, indeed, enslave us

Somethings exhibit a "genuine" need
While other things expose our lust

Somethings will make us well
And somethings will make us ill

Somethings are made to cure the world
While other things are made to kill

Lightning Bug #66

Contrary to popular opinion, I am not a judge. Consequently, I am a sensitized revolutionary tool/instrument, designed to compute, examine, and measure the magnitude and objective mode of evident spirits forthwith pending "The Judgement."

ALL GLORY

I can do nothing to impress GOD
Because, He is the "Master" of my skills

I am designed by Him, "For His Good Glory"
And, blessed to do His Will

I cannot boast or sound a trumpet
While carrying out His duties

For, HE "ALONE"
Deserves the "WORSHIP"

The "HONOR"
And the "BEAUTY"

                              AMEN

Lightning Bug #39

I'm a "SELL OUT" for Salvation.

AFFINITY

When you are feeling worthless
Un-necessary, or perhaps, even Suicidal

Bypass that spirit
PLEAD THE BLOOD OF JESUS
And burst free from the enemy's Bridle

The road to Righteousness is trod
With "much trembling and prayer"

So, just stay in cahoots with the Holy Ghost
BECAUSE JESUS IS THE demon SLAYER

Lightning Bug #26

Delight yourself in the Lord, and He will inspire you to great heights of victorious jubilation.

FOWL PLAY

My foe pretended
To be my friend

Then, stealthily conspired
To bring about my bitter END

I was needy
Lonely, and gullible

So, that "fake" projected an image
Of someone who was kind and loveable

But, when Jesus caught wind
To that "illusionist's" plan of lust

He REBUKED that spirit
And nullified its thrust

Lightning Bug #108

GOD is a force to be RECONCILED with.

MIRROR MIRROR

Without giving it a second thought, some of us become so desperate, or get so caught up in accomplishing our own goals, living our own dreams, and satifying our own ambitious appetite; that we just forge ahead in our endeavor, turning a blind eye, existing in a mental state of rivalry and denial, refusing to acknowledge the other beings, who unknowingly; therefore, unwillingly get pulled into an episode of events that sometimes are unproductive and injurious to the unsuspecting victim or victims. Many lives are unfavorably altered; oftentimes, terminated for the sake of another being's dream or ambition. One appears to be honored, while the other appears to be dishonored. Thus, leaving a false sense of importance in the minds of the participants and on-lookers. In this juncture lies the infraction that trigger the feeling of animosity. One subject has cause to celebrate; but, the other subject is left with a severe case of the "IF I WOULD OF, COULD OF" blues. The latter is left feeling used, abused, neglected, and mocked. Now, comes the feeling of being victimized and scandalized; meanwhile, "THE BAND PLAYS ON."

The one dreamer cannot, with all sincerity, share in the other's new-found joy, because of the over-whelming grief of self. The receiver of the joy is so busy celebrating, that the second infraction occurs; due to the brazen apathy of the satified dreamer. It seems that we are, somehow, mirror images of each other, so to speak, pawns that are used as a sacrifice for each other's dream, ambition, and circumstantial dilemma. We are driven by the over-whelming desire to survive with a minimum amount of inconvenience and discomfort. If we could conceive the side-effects, or the aftermath of some of our adventures, we probably would not pursue them so vigorously. Anytime is the right time for GOD'S INTERVENTION. Situations can become catastrophic. That is all the more reason why we must join forces, seek out our Creator, and pray for His Divine Intervention. In order for us to tap into real power, we have to be of one-mind – THE MIND OF GOD. We must practice Patience, Mercy, Forgiveness, and Understanding. NOW IS THE TIME. As eerie as it may be, what we do to others, we, somehow, also do to ourselves. Subsequently, when we try to understand others, we, then, can truly began to understand ourselves.

Lightning Bug #72

I Confess: "I am guilty of being so caught up in such a compromising position that I have began using my temple for the soul purpose of Aiding and Abetting the Holy Spirit."

IT'S JUST A PHASE

I perceive that your heart has been shattered
Therefore, it is not in just one piece

So, that explains your fickleness
Your desparate acts and exaggerated speech

Although, the open wounds are infected
And ooze of insecurity, impatience, and bitterness

I'm praying for your complete recovery
And soothing from the wilderness

Lightning Bug #78

It doesn't pay to spend too much time being excited about life; because, in the long run, it will only cost you.

SPACED OUT

GOD would like to "invite" YOU
To ATTEND
And WITNESS
His EXISTENCE

ANYONE
Who is anyone
Should not decline
Or, attempt to "resist" THIS

Truly, there is nothing
That could possibly be more GRAND
Than the chance to UNITE and PARLAY
With the Creator-in-Command

There isn't any dress code
Imposed on any of the guest
It's simply "Open House"
Of course, with the exception of all "flesh"

It is GUARANTEED
To be the EVENT of a LIFETIME
But, check your ego in
At the door

GOD is all consuming
Every knee SHALL
Traditionally "bow down"
And, bones SHALL tremble on the floor

JESUS Got Game
And GOD Got Skills
Meet the Master-of-Ceremonies
And the Host of "Thrill"

It is deemed Healthier
Than any "vitamin"
Or, regiment of "exercise"
Performed on a regular basis

Come one
Come All
Join the fold
The CREATOR isn't a sexist or a racist

Lightning Bug #74

The rewards of vanity
Are not greater than
The rewards of sanity

TRUCE

Lord, I need you to "earnestly"
Watch my back

Because, friends can be shady
And, even, family can be "wack"

So, I thought I would "rap"
This prayer to you

Requesting "protection"
And 'mercy," too

Lightning Bug #101

Don't keep it on the "Down Lo." Our Creator's death was staged.
GOD LIVES!

JESUS

JESUS is the PRINCE of PEACE
He died so we could live

All power and love is due Him
Because of who He is

WORTHY is the LAMB of GOD
Bless Him all you nations

Let His name be lifted up
On all television and radio stations

"Peace to Him" and "Glory to God"
Is what we should be saying

Instead of cursing and hating one another
Let us all consider "PRAYING"

Lightning Bug #88

"Four" Play to the "Derailment" of the Love train:

1. Over-indulgence
2. Jealousy
3. Conceit
4. Rage

HELLO, GOODBYE

As I travel through this world, do not hinder me; for, I am only on my way to join my Father, who has been weeping because he has missed me tremendously since I've been away. I was lost and temporarily blinded, and did not know my way back home. I've been tortured, scared, and put to shame. Only my Father can provide me with the proper care I need to heal. I am tired and very weak. I have to make it back home before the next storm comes my way. I cannot stop to play with you, or to fight with you; because, my father has found me, and commands me to come home. I must obey. For, He is my Father, my Creator, my Master, and my Friend.

Lightning Bug #46

Portraits of energy
Captured in time

Are episodes of life
That quicken the mind

THE PARADE

Trying to WALK IN THE SPIRIT
Through a parade of flesh
Can be a "gruesome" task
That appears to be "lonely" at BEST

RANTING and RAVING
Like an animal that has rabies
Is the HIGHLIGHT
Of the "mock" victory performance

Marked by the "razzle-dazzle"
And the smug feeling that one gets
When one is surrounded
In all of the adornment

A band Hurtling insults
While Marching in Formation
Is the "THEME"
For the Grand Finale

But, God is also in the audience
The sanctioned rain will fall
And put a damper on the parade
Down in the valley

You are not the FIRST
To be ushered
Up to the front
REMEMBER

JESUS
Paved the way
When He was FIRST called
To go up "ON-POINT"

GOD IS ALWAYS IN CONTROL
So, don't believe the HYPE
Just keep focusing on SALVATION
Cause, Satan isn't "Really" any SOUL'S Type

Lightning Bug #89

Doesn't it seem strange that the "price tag" the world places on "acceptance" is sometimes so expensive that, by the time one is finish paying the balance of it, there's nothing left of one's self to be accepted.

TATTLETALE

I'm going to tell God
My side of the story
And, I HOPE
He will reconsider

I'm going to throw my soul
On the mercy of His court
And, I PRAY
That He won't be bitter

I'm going to tell God
How "naïve" I was
And, that my "intellect"
Wasn't grounded or padded

My PERCEPTION
Was INCOHERENT and COERCED
Because, the basicity of KNOWLEDGE
Had not, yet, been added

I'm going to tell God
That the "insult" He suffered
Was not, as suggested, PREMEDITATED
Nor, was I trying to be vain

APPARENTLY
I was set up for failure
INEVITABLY
I loss more than I gained

I apologize for all the calamity
Stemming from my "major" infraction
I simply wasn't equipped to forego "testing"
Or, "prep" for interaction

Since I don't have the POWER
To reverse the deed
I can only HOPE
That God will accept my plea

I'm going to tell God
I need More of His STRENGTH
More of His WISDOM
And More of His WIT

The enemy's tactics seem relentless
SPORTING "spite" and "antagonizing rage"
Bent on snuffing out THE TRUTH
With its Smoke & Mirrors' craze

I'm going to tell God
That I've been "mortified"
DESTITUTE
And, that my "raw" emotions have been tossed

The "RING" LEADER
Continues to FEAST on my "perishable" flesh
While using my GRIEF
To serve as his floss

Lightning Bug #38

Imagination and "infatuation" can intrigue and "confuse" the senses, with "whimsical" hope and "figurative" dimensions.

A SERVANT'S REQUEST

Dear God

Bestow unto me
A prosperous spirit
And deter all murderers and thieves

Who seek to undermine your Blessings
With their Envy and their Greed

Instill in me the wisdom
To characterize Righteous decisions

To avoid all the snares of the enemy
And escape from the web of its prisons

Anoint me with the fruit of the spirit
So that I won't be a "control-freak"
Or, a 'snob"

Bless my comings
And Bless my goings
To fulfill a Holy Ghost's job

Lord, I hope I'm not being to forward
But, be my doctor
If you will

In JESUS' name
I ask these things

Because, it is He
Who has paid the bill

Lightning Bug #100

TREAT yourself. Fall in love with God; He deserves it.

Lightning Bug #70

The positives and the negatives
The pros and the cons

The peasant and the deity
Are like the sea and the pond

Lightning Bug #30

What is, and what is expected
Hovers over intentions

Thoughts are caught between the waves
Of pre-calculated dimensions

Lightning Bug #93

Being "arrogant" miraculously allows a person to become immune to criticism; even "constructed" criticism!

Lightning Bug #97

The Holy Spirit is my MENTOR.

Lightning Bug #98

Phenomenonally, bullies do not always function as diabolical barriers. To the contrary; they also function as laxatives that produce the "Growing Pains" that result in a "Royal Flush" of future gains.

Lightning Bug #81

How much space is allotted for diversity in a "uni" verse?

Lightning Bug #99

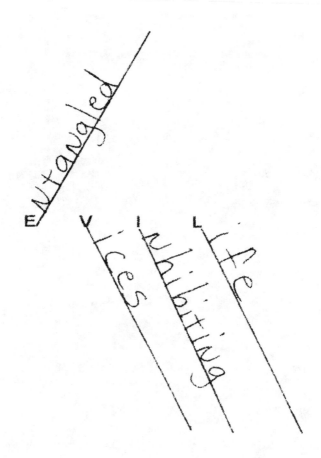

Lightning Bug #55

NOTICE: All "Flattery-Stricken" Victims

Please report for "exorcism"

(Under the Blood of Jesus)

ASAP

Lightning Bug #6

When you refuse to let your conscience be your guide, you deny "The Power of Love;" because evil dictates on the other side.

Lightning Bug #77

The sky is blue because it is God's "Blueprint" of His world; and when the clouds turn gray, it is an indication that there is a shift change in effect amongst His maintenance crew.

Lightning Bug #76

The "smirk" of a smile
Coupled with a "pretentious style"

Are "spiteful" attributions

That "constitute" the affirmation
Of a "deceptive" resolution

Lightning Bug #73

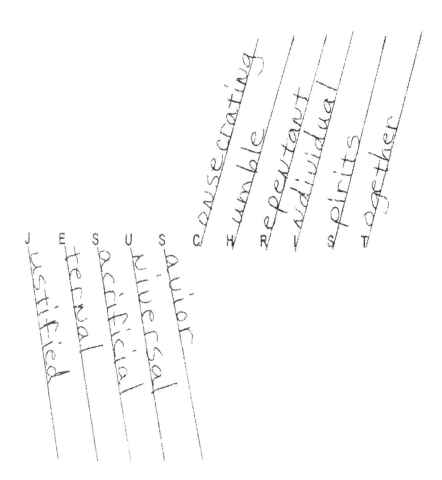

Lightning Bug #64

Don't be too shy to "Bare" your soul in front of God. After-all, it's not like He hasn't seen it before.

Lightning Bug #68

"To The Victor, Go The Spoils"

If the term "spoil" implies such factors as "damage," "ruin," "decay/rot;" then, does it also stand to reason that those, who "enjoy the spoils of war," have taken on the personification of vultures?

Lightning Bug #65

Lightning Bug #104

Scholastically speaking: We are all tools of a trade.

For example; some of us function as tables and chairs, some of us function as pads and pencils, some of us function as paste and glues, some of us function as paints and brushes, some of us function as erasers and scissors, some of us function as rulers and pencil sharpeners, and some of us function as a compass; and together, we form a vivid pictorial view for God.

Lightning Bug #103

JESUS is anti-arrogant.

THE "SIN" DECAYED PROPOSAL

As the situation stands, we are all bound together by sin and are, therefore, each other's prisoner. Henceforth; it appears that the only means of survival presented in such an ordeal, is for us to earnestly start conducting ourselves, somewhat, like Siamese twins. We start by changing our menu and diet by serving Humble Pie for breakfast, lunch, and dinner (no in-between-meal snacks included). Secondly, tolerate and bear each other's burden. Thirdly, appreciate each other, and fourth; but contrarily foremost, pray for mercy with each other and for each other.

Lightning Bug #102

As one travels through time bartering, haggling, sacrificing, and gambling with life, while at the same time, desiring to be loved, idolized, or remembered by the world; one must realize this "hardfast" guideline or rule that comes with that territory:

> "Boasting" and "Showing-Off" can either "make" you or "break" you; but, when the two turn delirious or wear-out-their-welcome, one must take a break to re-group by returning to the Potter's mold for a re-make.

Lightning Bug #54

Coping with "hope" vs. dope
Is a "sobering" transition, "No Doubt"

But, the sacrifice
Of such an endeavor

Will promote healing
From the inside-out

Lightning Bug #79

Traces of residue from the "fallout" of sin will oftentimes prompt a contaminated individual to seek shelter and cleansing under the wings of "The Almighty God." Lest, he perish in the meltdown.

Lightning Bug #112

God collects tears, and turns them into MIRACLES!

Lightning Bug #111

I'm Jesus' "side-kick."

A PRAYER FOR THE WORLD

Almighty God

Forgive us for our sins
Have mercy upon us
In Jesus' name

Bless thy Holiness
Be *praised, glorified, worshipped*
And sought after by your creation
For-ever-more, eternally
In Jesus' name

Bless this nation
Keep us safe
And in thy *will*
In Jesus' name

Thank you
For thy many *blessings*

Bless all our neighbors
To the *North, East, West*
And *South* of us
That thy *will* be done
Thy kingdom come
In Jesus' name

Bless all creatures
Both big and small
That thy *will* be done
In Jesus' name

Bless the sick
And bless the *well*
That thy *will* be done
In Jesus' name

Bless all thy *creation*
Have MERCY on us all
In Jesus' name
AMEN

Notice

"FREE"

Prosperity
Proficiency
Test

Sponsored by:

"FUTURE"
ENTERPRISE
INC.

Please consult with your parents, doctor/psychiatrist, guidance counselor, or spiritual leader before taking this test.

Disinterested/Burned-Out students needed for "FUN"damental Testing.

CAUTION: If you are allergic to schools, pens/pencils, writing paper, or teachers, please be advised that reading further could be "Dangerous" (In severe cases, "Fatal") to your

ATTITUDE!!

Please Note: If you are beginning to feel irritated, confused, or mentally challenged, please follow this antidote:

1. Take a deep breath and exhale slowly.

2. Deflate ego with a "Reality" check (reality checks are free of charge, and can be found in any local unemployment line or prison).

3. Rush to nearest full-length mirror to correct your body language and facial expression.

4. Take one "Chill" pill with 8 oz glass of orange juice (WARNING - larger dosages of "Chill" pills have been known to cause sluggishness and loss of memory in some students).

*If symptoms persist for more than 48 hours, seek professional tutoring immediately at your local educational facility.

Test-ready students can now start: Please take your time and "THINK."

Question: What is a four-letter word that rhymes with "FAIL"

Answer_____

Clue: Profanity is not included in this test, and is considered to be an automatic failure.

Comprehension

Directions: **Please read, memorize, and define the following words:**

(1)

```
"R   E   A   D   I   N   G"
    E   N   C   I   N   O   O
    N   A   H   S   T   T   O
    E   B   I   C   E   A   D
    W   L   E   O   L   B   N
        E   V   V   L   L   E
            E   E   E   E   S
                R   C       S
                    T
                    U
                    A
                    L
```

(2)

```
"W   R   I   T   I   N   G"
    I   E   N   O   N   E   O
    S   G   T   W   N   E   N
    D   E   E   A   O   D   E
    O   N   G   R   C   S
    M   E   R   D   E
        R   I   S   N
        A   T       T
        T   Y
        E
        S
```

(3)

```
"A   R   I   T   H   M   E   T   I   C"
    R   E   N   A   A   E   N   H   N   O
    T   S   T   C   R   N   E   R   N   M
    I   P   R   K   M   T   R   O   O   M
    C   O   I   F   O   A   G   U   V   U
    U   N   G   U   N   L   Y   G   A   N
    L   S   U   L   I       H   T   I
    A   E   E       O       O   I   T
    T   S   S       U       U   N   I
    E               S       T   G   E
                                    S
```

STOP! TEST ENDS

229

Our Mission is Accomplished
Thank you, for
your "TIME"

Please Note: If you are experiencing signs of exhaustion or frustration
after taking this test, please do the following exercise:

Walk (do not run) to your nearest library or bookstore to obtain an
updated dictionary. After you have done so, please feel free to take one
more "Chill" pill with 1/2 (one-half) glassful of vegetable juice and
"PEACE-OUT."

Printed in the United States
77918LV00005B/142-159